GW00692008

Stretch yourself in
many directions.

'I've met many thinkers and many cats, but the wisdom of cats is infinitely superior'

Hippolyte Taine

FELINE PHILOSOPHY

Summersdale Publishers Ltd
46 West Street
Chichester
West Sussex
PO19 1RP
UK

www.summersdale.com

Printed and bound in Belgium

ISBN 1 84024 454 2

Feline
Philosophy

Life Lessons From Your Cat

Mike Hatt

summersdale

Listen to others, but also
listen to yourself.

Be grateful for your daily food. If you're not hungry, you can always play with it.

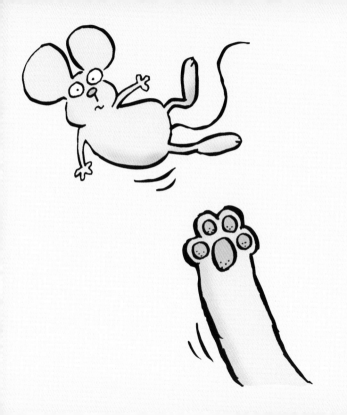

It's OK to have a
dull coat – it's the tiger
within that counts.

But there's no reason
to be seen with a hair
out of place.

Always be ready to
share a plate of food.

If you don't like
the look of it, shred it.

Be hard to
say goodbye to...

... but easy to
come back to.

Take charge of your
surroundings — kick
away the dead leaves,
stalk the magpies...
but don't forget to
enjoy the butterflies.

Make friends with
people in high places
however you can.

Be curious –
you can afford to
lose a life or two.

When in need, don't be afraid to ask a friend.

Stare unabashedly –
no one ever got anything
by being coy.

Seek out the
sunny places.

Don't always come
when you are called.
Good things come to
those who wait.

Slow down; make
time to eat the flowers.

Sometimes you just have
to leap without looking.

Don't be shy
about sharing
your achievements.

If someone steps
on your paws, let
them know...

… but after a cuddle
and an apology,
forgive and forget.

Take the best seat in the
house; your contentment
is as important as
the next fellow's.

Embrace signs
of maturity – flaunt
your hair loss.

Not everything in life
can be explained.

Go barefoot among
the buttercups.

See the possibilities
in everything.

Public displays of
affection make the
world a happier place.

Follow your instincts.

If the sun is no longer
shining on you, move
to another spot.

Choose your
friends wisely.

Don't waste time trying
to please everybody.

Always make
time for play.

Contentment can't
be bought.

Take the initiative –
if you don't ask
you don't get.

You can live
without television.

There is no place so
dark that comfort
cannot be found.

Sometimes you are
just in a bad mood —
there's no need
to explain yourself.

Don't hold back – yawn
like you really mean it.

Be there for
your friends.

Take it slow; the faster you run, the more likely you are to forget where you're going.

Be independent, but it's OK to depend on others sometimes.

You can't blame
everything on the dog.

When in doubt, act like
you're in the right.

Be a good listener.

Right now, there is at least one person who can't wait to see you.

Spilled milk isn't always
something to cry over.

Feel free to speak out
when something makes
you unhappy.

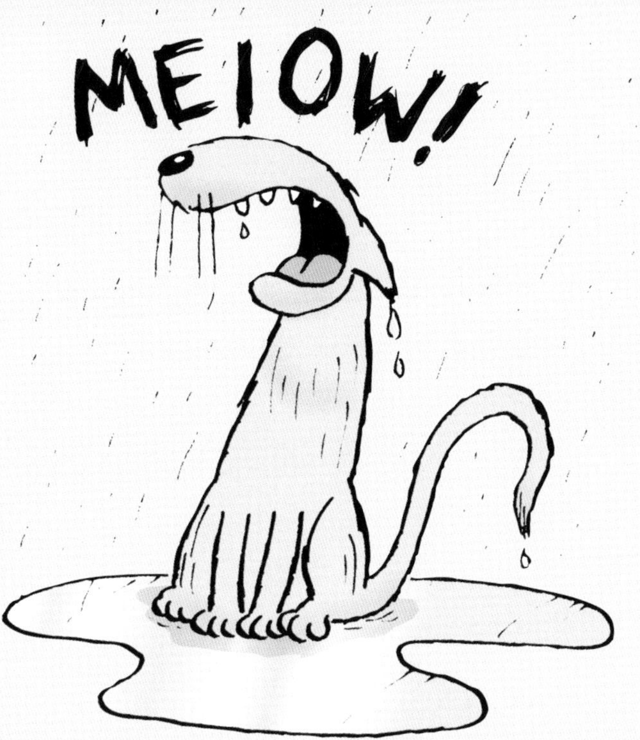
MEIOW!

If you feel like climbing to the top of the shed, climb to the top of the shed.

There's nothing better
than finding a good
lap to curl up in.

If in doubt, sleep on it.

Tread lightly
on this earth.

Don't give away all your
secrets. Be cool
and mysterious.

Everyone is entitled to change their mind.

Don't be a slave
to the telephone.

Do what you want,
when you want.

Learn to see what
you need even when
it's all gone dark.

Keep climbing until you reach the very top of the curtains.

Don't be afraid to
take chances and
try new things.

Be tolerant, but
don't be a pushover.

Don't let a closed door
stand in your way.

To err is human.
To forgive, feline.

Other cat books from Summersdale

The More I See of Men, the More I Love My Cat

Daisy Hay

£4.99 Hb

1 84024 421 6

Cats are better than men: fact. When was the last time you had to tell a cat not to embarrass you in public? Would a cat go out for a night on the tiles and come back smelling of anything worse than a fish supper? All the evidence is inside this book: there's nothing mad about being a catwoman.

Daisy Hay lives with many cats – and no residential men.

Cats

Quotes and Stuff

£4.99 Hb

1 84024 371 6

'Thousands of years ago, cats were worshipped as gods. Cats have never forgotten this.'

Bursting at the seams with quotes, poems, jokes and stories, this book is a delightful celebration of the world's favourite furry friend.

The purrfect gift for every cat-lover.

www.summersdale.com